S0-BZA-545

Therese M. Shea

# ZENDAYA
## ACTRESS AND SINGER

**Enslow Publishing**
101 W. 23rd Street
Suite 240
New York, NY 10011
USA
enslow.com

# WORDS TO KNOW

**diverse**  Made up of people or things that are different from each other.

**finale**  The last show.

**hula**  A Hawaiian dance.

**influential**  Being able to have an effect.

**nominate**  To suggest for an honor.

**producer**  A person who is in charge of making a play, movie, or record.

**racism**  Treating people poorly or unfairly because of their race.

**trapeze**  A short bar that is hung high above the ground by two ropes. A circus performer does tricks on it.

# CONTENTS

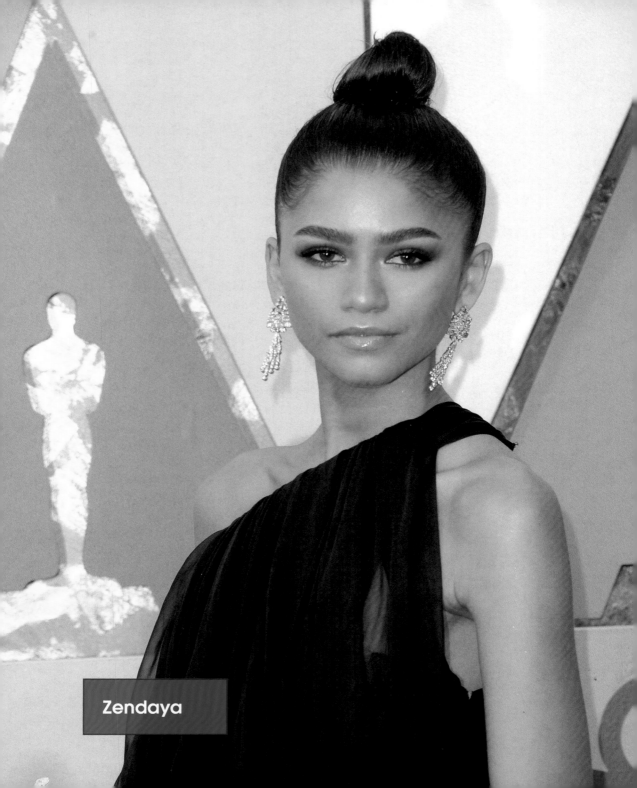

Zendaya

# CHAPTER 1
# A TRIPLE THREAT

When people meet Zendaya (pronounced zehn-DAY-ah), they're amazed at how talented she is. She is what is known as a triple threat. She dances, she sings, and she acts. But the young star also has other interests. She works to fight racism and encourages young people to have a healthy body image. She uses her fame to make people aware of her causes.

Zendaya Says:

"For me, I get a mixture of all the worlds . . . I have my African first name, I have a middle name that is [my mom's] middle name, which is French, but we did it African spelling, so it's literally me in a name."

Zendaya poses with her parents. Her name means "to give thanks" in the language of the Shona people of Zimbabwe.

## A SHY CHILD

Zendaya Maree Stoermer was born on September 1, 1996, in Oakland, California. Her parents are Kazembe Ajamu Coleman and Claire Stoermer. Zendaya was a very shy child. She even had to repeat kindergarten because of her shyness. But the quiet little girl loved to perform in front of people!

## GETTING ON STAGE

Zendaya's mother was the stage manager at a theater. Young Zendaya spent a lot of time there. She performed in its youth program and had parts in some shows. She was also in a dance group and enjoyed dancing hula.

Zendaya attended the Oakland School for the Arts. She also trained with the American Conservatory Theater. She modeled and acted in commercials, too.

In 2010, Zendaya got her big break. She beat out about 200 girls to get a part on the Disney Channel series *Shake It Up*. She played the role of Raquel "Rocky" Blue. She and costar Bella Thorne performed songs for the show. It was a hit!

Zendaya and her *Shake It Up* costar, Bella Thorne. The two played backup dancers on a television show.

7

For one commercial, Zendaya performed as a backup dancer for another future star, Selena Gomez.

## ROLE MODEL

When Zendaya was sixteen, the Disney Channel asked her to be in another show: *Super Awesome Katey*. Zendaya would play a teen spy. But she decided she wanted a say in this show. She asked to be a **producer**. She wanted the show to have more **diverse** characters. She was also behind the show changing its name to *K.C. Undercover*.

Zendaya wanted her character to be unique and strong. K.C. was a math genius who was great at martial arts. Zendaya was proud to help create a character of color who was a role model.

# CHAPTER 2
# SINGING AND DANCING STAR

Zendaya is not just a talented actor. She started her singing career in 2009 with the *Kidz Bop* albums. She signed a recording deal with Hollywood Records in 2012. She released her first album the next year. It was called *Zendaya.* She performed concerts around the United States.

## MAKING MUSIC

In February 2016, Zendaya released the song "Something New," with Chris Brown. It was **nominated** for Best Song at the Teen Choice Awards. Fans can't wait for Zendaya's

Zendaya Says:

**"I have so many friends who say yes to everything or feel like they can't stand up for themselves in a situation. No: You *have* the power."**

Zendaya sings the national anthem at a Dodgers game in 2013.

next album. She says she wants to take her time making music. "I'm kind of creating my own music and I'm kind of creating my own zone, my own lane as an artist," she explains.

## DANCING TO A NEW BEAT

In 2013, Zendaya went on the TV competition *Dancing with the Stars*. Her partner was professional dancer Val Chmerkovskiy. Zendaya had a dance background and played a dancer on *Shake It Up*. But the competition

On *Dancing with the Stars*, Zendaya and Val Chmerkovskiy dedicated a dance to her grandmother, who had breast cancer at the time.

wasn't easy for her since she was mostly used to hip-hop. She was also the youngest person ever to enter the competition. Still, she made the **finale**! They didn't win, but it was a great experience for Zendaya.

Zendaya has made guest appearances on TV shows such as *A.N.T. Farm* and *Good Luck Charlie*.

In 2016, Zendaya landed her first movie role. She played Michelle in the movie *Spider-Man: Homecoming*. As she did in *K.C. Undercover*, Zendaya added her own ideas to the character. She decided that Michelle would not wear makeup and would carry tea around with her.

The film was a success with critics and audiences. It made over $880 million! Although she was not the star of the movie, Zendaya won a 2017 Teen Choice Award for Choice Summer Movie Actress.

Zendaya Says:

"There were a lot of opportunities that came my way that would not have been the right choice . . . But I wanted to do quality projects, cool things that made me excited, and I didn't care if I only had one line."

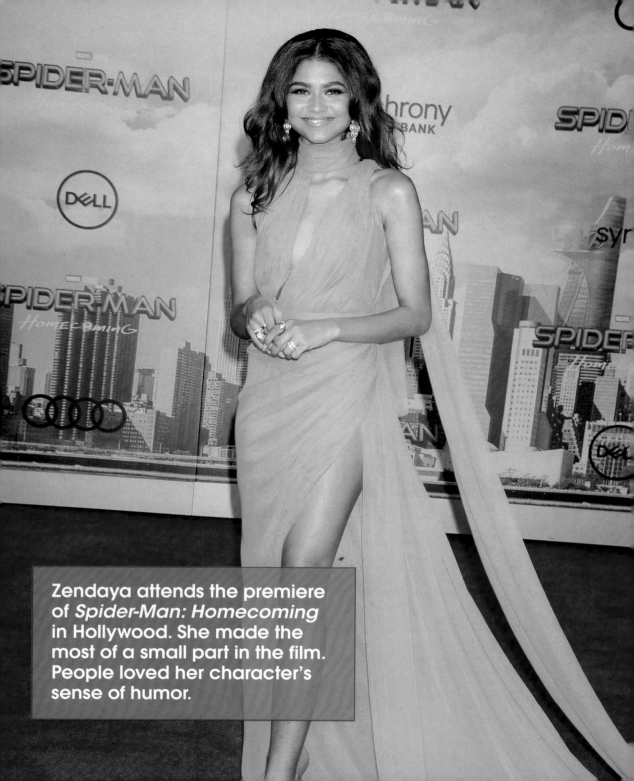

Zendaya attends the premiere of *Spider-Man: Homecoming* in Hollywood. She made the most of a small part in the film. People loved her character's sense of humor.

## FROM SPIDER-MAN TO SHOWMAN

Just a few months after *Spider-Man* was released, Zendaya got a lead role in another major movie: *The Greatest Showman*. It was a musical, which was not a problem for Zendaya. "I've been in love with musicals since I was a kid," she said.

Zendaya starred as Anne Wheeler with Hugh Jackman and Zac Efron. Anne was a trapeze artist in the circus. Zendaya was offered a stunt double. But she chose to do

In 2013, Zendaya came out with a book called *Between U and Me*. She wrote it to help young people going through their tween and teen years.

Zendaya performs in *The Greatest Showman* with her costar, Zac Efron.

all the trapeze work herself. Michael Gracey, the film's director said, "I would shout out a direction or give the slightest adjustment, and while flying through the air, she'd do it." She also recorded music for the movie, including the song "Rewrite the Stars."

# CHAPTER 4

# FASHION ICON AND ROLE MODEL

When Zendaya was just eighteen, she was invited to attend the Academy Awards. She chose to wear a striking white dress. She wore her hair in long dreadlocks. Most of the fashion world fell in love with her. But one television commentator made an unkind remark about her hairstyle.

When she heard it, Zendaya was angry. Still, she reacted calmly. She wrote a letter and placed it on her Instagram account. In it, she named a number of respected people of color who wear their hair in locs. She said, "My wearing my hair in locs on an Oscar red carpet was to showcase them in a positive light, to remind people of color that our hair is good enough."

Zendaya has more than 46 million followers on Instagram.

Zendaya made a splash at the 2015 Academy Awards.

## HELPING OTHERS

Zendaya has become a role model. In 2015, she was named one of *Time* magazine's top influential teens. She said, "I am really proud of the fact that I'm able to use people knowing my name and knowing who I am for good things."

Every year, Zendaya spends her birthday doing charity work. She works with a group called Convoy of Hope. It provides food around the world for those who need it. For her eighteenth birthday, she asked her fans to help her raise money for poor children in Haiti, Tanzania, and the Philippines.

Zendaya Says:

"To me locs are a symbol of strength and beauty, almost like a lion's mane."

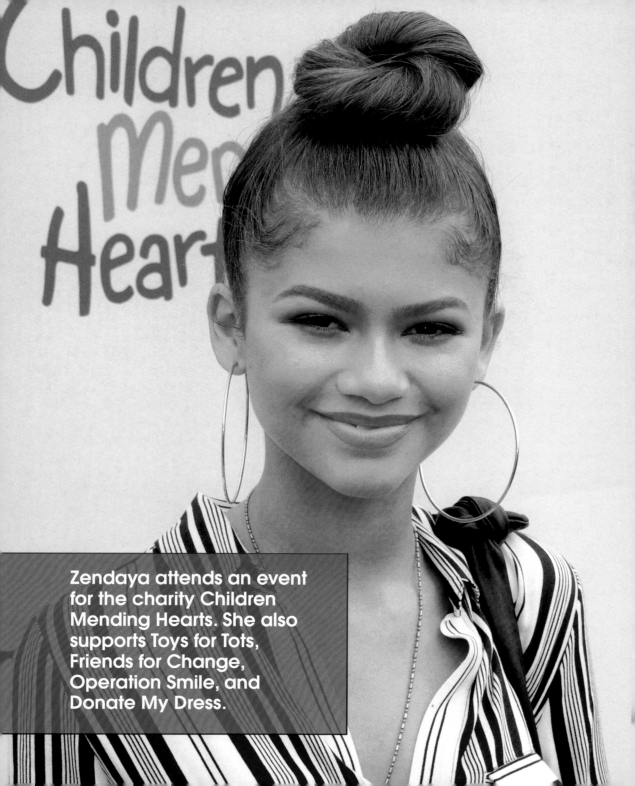

Zendaya attends an event for the charity Children Mending Hearts. She also supports Toys for Tots, Friends for Change, Operation Smile, and Donate My Dress.

In 2017, for her twenty-first birthday, Zendaya did not celebrate with a wild party. She said she did not feel the need to drink alcohol and wanted to focus on her work. That year, she chose to raise money for the victims of Hurricane Harvey.

Zendaya realizes that she has had a very full life for such a young person. She says: "It's been an amazing ride. . . . I'm proud of what I've accomplished, but there's so much more to do." What will this rising star do next?

# TIMELINE

1996   Zendaya is born on September 1 in Oakland, California.

2010   Lands the role of Rocky Blue on Disney's *Shake It Up*.

2012   Signs a recording deal with Hollywood Records.

2013   Is a runner up on *Dancing with the Stars*.
          Releases her first album, *Zendaya*, in September.

2015   Attends the Academy Awards wearing dreadlocks.
          *K.C. Undercover* begins.

2016   Starts a clothing line called Daya by Zendaya.

2017   Appears as Michelle in the movie *Spider-Man: Homecoming*.
          Wins a Teen Choice Award for Choice Summer Movie Actress.
          Appears as a trapeze artist in *The Greatest Showman*.

## BOOKS

Caravantes, Peggy. *Zendaya: Star Performer*. Mankato, MN: The Child's World, 2018.

Orr, Nicole. *Zendaya*. Kennett Square, PA: Purple Toad Publishing, 2018.

Zendaya, and Sheryl Berk. *Between U and Me: How to Rock Your Tween Years with Style and Confidence*. New York, NY: Disney Hyperion Books, 2013.

## WEBSITES

**Zendaya**
*www.imdb.com/name/nm3918035/*
Check out Zendaya's page to see her upcoming movie roles.

**Zendaya**
*zendaya.com*
This is Zendaya's official site.

**Zendaya Coleman**
*www.biography.com/people/zendaya-coleman-21219049*
Read a short biography of Zendaya.

# INDEX

Published in 2019 by Enslow Publishing, LLC.
101 W. 23rd Street, Suite 240, New York, NY 10011

Copyright © 2019 by Enslow Publishing, LLC.
All rights reserved.

No part of this book may be reproduced by any means without the written permission of the publisher.

**Library of Congress Cataloging-in-Publication Data**

Names: Shea, Therese, author.
Title: Zendaya : actress and singer / Therese M. Shea.
Description: New York : Enslow Publishing, 2019. | Series: Junior biographies | Includes bibliographical references and index. | Audience: Grades 3-5.
Identifiers: LCCN 2018002546| ISBN 9781978502093 (library bound) | ISBN 9781978503090 (pbk.) | ISBN 9781978503106 (6 pack)
Subjects: LCSH: Zendaya, 1996- —Juvenile literature. | Actors—United States–Biography—Juvenile literature. | Singers—United States—Biography—Juvenile literature. | Models (Persons)—United States—Biography—Juvenile literature.
Classification: LCC PN2287.Z47 S54 2019 | DDC 791.4302/8092 [B] –dc23
LC record available at https://lccn.loc.gov/2018002546

Printed in the United States of America

**To Our Readers:** We have done our best to make sure all website addresses in this book were active and appropriate when we went to press. However, the author and the publisher have no control over and assume no liability for the material available on those websites or on any websites they may link to. Any comments or suggestions can be sent by email to customerservice@enslow.com.

**Photos Credits:** Cover, p. 1 Don Arnold/WireImage/Getty Images; pp. 2, 3, 22, 23, 24, back cover (curves graphic) Alena Kazlouskaya/Shutterstock.com; p. 4 Tinseltown/Shutterstock.com; p. 6 Bill McCay/WireImage/Getty Images; p. 7 © AP Images; p. 10 Mark Sullivan/WireImage/Getty Images; p. 11 Debra L Rothenberg/Getty Images; p. 14 Frank Trapper/Corbis Entertainment/Getty Images; p. 16 Collection Christophel/Alamy Stock Photo; p. 18 Jason Merritt/Getty Images; p. 20 Jon Kopaloff/FilmMagic/Getty Images; interior page bottoms (lights) Smart Design /Shutterstock.com.